TYPE
NINE

The Peacemaker, Mediator, Reconciler

Inspiring | Educating | Creating | Entertaining

Brimming with creative inspiration, how-to projects, and useful information to enrich your everyday life, quarto.com is a favorite destination for those pursuing their interests and passions.

© 2022 Quarto Publishing Group USA Inc.
Text © 2022 Carver and Green

First Published in 2022 by Fair Winds Press, an imprint of The Quarto Group, 100 Cummings Center, Suite 265-D, Beverly, MA 01915, USA.
T (978) 282-9590 F (978) 283-2742 www.quarto.com

Fair Winds Press titles are also available at discount for retail, wholesale, promotional, and bulk purchase. For details, contact the Special Sales Manager by email at specialsales@quarto.com or by mail at The Quarto Group, Attn: Special Sales Manager, 100 Cummings Center, Suite 265-D, Beverly, MA 01915, USA.

ISBN: 978-0-7603-7673-7

Cover Image and Illustration: Liz Carver
Page Layout: Megan Jones Design

ENNEATYPE 9
THE PEACEMAKER, MEDIATOR, RECONCILER

An Interactive Workbook

Liz Carver and Josh Green

FAIR WINDS

CONTENTS

INTRODUCTION

Welcome to the type NINE enneaguide! This book is designed to help you ask deeper questions of yourself, your motivations, your coping strategies, and more. We always say that knowing your type is the first step, and the real work begins after that. Knowing your type is information, and digging deeper to ask harder questions is the start of transformation.

You can go through this enneaguide at whatever pace suits you best. Some questions will be easy for you to answer off the top of your head. Others will require you to sit and think for a minute. Some may even require you to sit with them for a few days or more. Sometimes you'll be prompted to go do something in real life and then reflect on that experience. To that end, there are spaces in this book for you to interact with these prompts and questions. The goal isn't to simply finish this book and move on to the next thing. Rather, the goal is for this book to be a tool to help you understand yourself better in relation to the world around you so you can live a fuller, more integrated life.

Feel free to invite loved ones who know you on this journey with you! They may be able to help you see things in your life that you have a hard time seeing for yourself. Remember that a healthier and more self-aware you is a gift to everyone in your life.

We hope that this enneaguide is enlightening, challenging, and encouraging for you. Enjoy your time walking through this guide!

— Liz and Josh

PART I

BEING A
TYPE NINE

In this section, we'll review some of the aspects of being a type NINE on a broad level so that you can refamiliarize yourself with some of the NINE language and what NINEs are like in general. There will be aspects that you identify with strongly, and there may be aspects that you don't identify with at all. Both are completely fine. The point isn't that we (Liz and Josh) completely understand you but that you have the space to understand yourself and have the words to identify how you are the way you are.

MOTIVATION

NINEs are generally motivated by a desire or a need to be in constant harmony with the world around them. This motivation has roots that are selfish and roots that are others-focused. The coping strategy that you as a NINE learn is to keep yourself away from any disturbances of your peace because any threat to your sense of peace and harmony is either too hard, too scary, or requires too much energy. NINEs strive to do what they please and are generally unbothered by life around them. However, at best, NINEs can be motivated to see true unity and harmony in the people and systems around them because they have a more natural bent toward seeking peace and unity.

➤ How does this motivation resonate with you?

_____

_____

_____

_____

_____

_____

_____

_____

➤ Are there aspects that you feel may be true for most NINEs but aren't true for you?

_____

_____

_____

_____

_____

_____

_____

_____

➤ How does this motivation feed your own ego? How does it actually help you? How does it actually help others?

_____

_____

_____

_____

_____

_____

_____

➤ Do you find it easy to say or claim what motivates you? If so, what else is motivating to you? If not, why do you have a hard time claiming these things?

_____

_____

_____

_____

_____

_____

_____

_____

THE SHADOW SIDE

Just as each type has a great gift to give to the world, each type also has their shadow side: the parts of their type that they're not exactly proud of. The shadow side is what we need to root out, unlearn, and grow beyond. Also called the core vice, or "deadly sin," the shadow side for NINEs is sloth. Sloth can take the form of physical laziness, in which NINEs let tasks pile up, watch too much TV, never leave their home, and so on. It can also take the form of more social or relational laziness, in which they withdraw or hibernate from their friends and community for extended times, not taking initiative or showing up, or getting too comfortable with a subpar status quo. In the pursuit of love and acceptance, NINEs tend to settle for a cease-fire or an absence of conflict.

> How would you describe your shadow side in your own words?

_____

_____

_____

_____

_____

_____

_____

_____

_____

> How does physical sloth/laziness show up for you?

_____

_____

_____

_____

_____

_____

_____

_____

_____

➤ How does social/relational laziness show up for you?

_____

_____

_____

_____

_____

_____

_____

➤ Describe a time when you settled for a cease-fire rather than facing the conflict that needed to be faced. What did you learn from that? In what ways did the old habits stay the same after that?

_____

_____

_____

_____

_____

_____

_____

_____

➤ If you were to engage in conflict rather than settle for a cease-fire, what would be the cost?

_____

_____

_____

_____

_____

_____

_____

NESTING LIES

IT'S NOT OKAY TO ASSERT MYSELF.

MY WANTS AND NEEDS DON'T MATTER.

KEEPING THE PEACE IS MORE IMPORTANT THAN I AM.

NOBODY SEES OR UNDERSTANDS ME.

I'M NOT SPECIAL.

INTEGRATION AND DISINTEGRATION

When NINEs are in moments or seasons of disintegration, they move toward SIX and take on SIX-like characteristics. Their usual calm and relaxed demeanor can become paranoid, anxious, and defensive. Their minds race with constant thoughts and fears rather than taking things slowly, as they usually do. The tendency to smooth out tension and extend the benefit of the doubt to others becomes more suspicious, and they assume the worst in others. The usual calm waters become very choppy and uneasy.

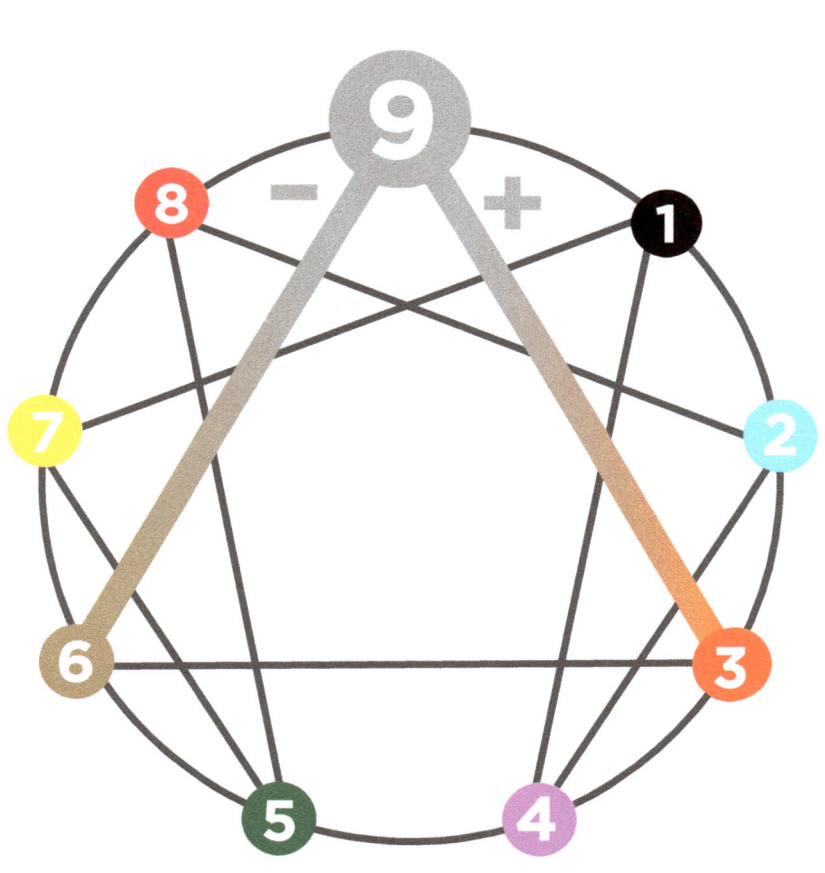

➤ Think back on a time when you weren't doing too well or were experiencing disintegration. How did you feel like you diverted from your normal way of being? Did you see any of the aforementioned signs of disintegration in yourself?

_____

_____

_____

_____

_____

_____

_____

_____

_____

WARNING SIGNS

**ANALYSIS PARALYSIS/
OVERTHINKING**

EASILY AGITATED

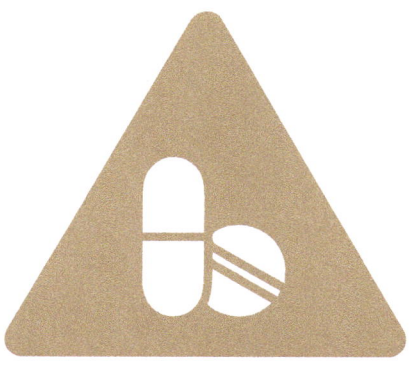

NARCOTIZING

NUMBING

PICKING FIGHTS

PARANOIA

WITHDRAWING

WORST·CASE·SCENARIO THINKING

When healthy and in seasons or moments of integration, NINEs move toward THREE and take on some of the better THREE-like characteristics. They become more attuned to the present moment and are more aware of what is needed of them in the future to achieve what they want or need. Integrated NINEs become quickly decisive and action-oriented. They stop withdrawing and start engaging. While NINEs are often asleep to many things around them, in times of integration, they are very alert and aware of their surroundings. They can take in a lot of information and use it to make good decisions.

➤ **Think of a time when you were healthy and integrated. It could have been a day or a more prolonged season. What positive changes did you notice? What parts of that experience do you long to become a more normal part of your life?**

_____

_____

_____

_____

_____

_____

_____

_____

_____

_____

ENNEADICTIONARY FOR NINES

Merging (v.): NINEs have a tendency to merge or become one with others, meaning they may find that they agreed or aligned with someone for the sake of peace when in fact they do not agree with this person. It can also look like agreeing to do an activity that they don't want to do or doing an activity the same way someone else does rather than how they'd do it themselves.

Inner Sanctum (n.): All of life is exhausting for a NINE, who is trying to maintain external and internal peace at all times, so they can be known to take little vacations into their minds, or their inner sanctum.

One-Hundred-Mile Stare (n.): NINEs sometimes give the impression of being absent-minded or slightly befuddled. If nothing is happening around them, they will check out. They can even suddenly fall asleep in broad daylight. The one-hundred-mile stare is when a NINE checks out midconversation.

Numbing/Narcotizing (n.): The defense mechanism of NINEs is to numb or narcotize through anything from watching videos online to staring into space, eating food, exercising, or using something more dangerous like drugs. Because they don't feel adequate for the many challenges of life, they may take refuge in some sort of behavior to distract them. NINEs seek these stimulants and strong sensations from the outside because they can find it difficult to stimulate themselves.

➤ Did any of these definitions particularly strike you? Is there anything that highly resonates with you?

_____

_____

_____

_____

_____

_____

_____

➤ Is there anything you strongly disagree with? What is it? How do you experience things differently?

_____

_____

_____

_____

_____

_____

_____

_____

➤ Ask a trusted friend to tell you the next time they see you doing the one-hundred-mile stare. How was that experience for you? What impact did it have on your self-awareness?

_____

_____

_____

_____

_____

_____

_____

➤ What are some things that you use to numb or distract yourself from the harder things in life? How do they keep you from engaging in the present moment?

_____

_____

_____

_____

_____

_____

_____

➤ Who are some people who can help you maintain your autonomy and avoid merging? Take some time to intentionally tell them that you're looking to grow out of merging behaviors. Practice telling them what you really think, what you really want, what you need to do, and so on. Write about your experience.

_____

_____

_____

_____

_____

_____

_____

_____

_____

ORIGIN STORIES/ CHILDHOOD WOUNDS

In this section, we will explore some common childhood wounds for NINEs. Please remember that these are not necessarily universal. You may relate to some aspects of the NINE origin stories very strongly and others not at all. If your experience is different, take the time to put into words how your experience was different from some of these common stories. Our aim is not to predict what sort of trauma you experienced growing up but rather to help you put into words how you came to have the patterns and coping mechanisms that NINEs have.

Growing up, did you:

- feel unimportant or lost in a group (maybe you were the oldest child and had to take care of some bigger personalities or you were one of many children) and your opinions weren't heard?

- feel overlooked, neglected, or overpowered?

- feel ignored or attacked for having needs or expressing yourself?

➤ **Does any of this resonate with you? None of it? All of it? Take some time to describe this part of your origin story.**

_____

_____

_____

_____

_____

_____

_____

_____

_____

_____

_____

_____

_____

Because of these experiences you just described, did you learn to:

- keep a low profile . . .
- focus on the needs/experiences of others . . .
- be easygoing and accommodating . . .
- detach yourself from the physical world in favor of a dream world . . .

. . . so that you could

- feel connected to others by accommodating the needs of others and denying your own needs?
- feel in control by erasing your needs/emotions from the equation to maintain peace and balance?

➤ **Which of these tendencies did you see forming in yourself while growing up? What was the reward or benefit of acting this way? What was the cost of doing the opposite?**

_____

_____

_____

_____

_____

_____

_____

_____

_____

➤ **Which (if any) of these statements did you believe as a child?**

- I don't matter as much as others do.
- If everyone else is fine, I'm fine.

_____

_____

_____

_____

_____

_____

_____

➤ **What would you go back and tell yourself as a child, if you could?**

_____

_____

_____

_____

_____

_____

_____

_____

PART II

DIGGING DEEPER AS A TYPE NINE

We hope that by now you have uncovered some ways that NINE-ness is showing up in you, whether in your shadow side or how you move to THREE in integration and SIX in disintegration. Maybe some of your coping strategies have been uncovered in your origin story.

In this next section, we want to dig deeper into some of the nuances of NINE-ness. The color for NINEs is gray, a neutral color, which makes sense for our peacemaking, neutral NINEs. They can relate to and empathize with both sides in any situation and are content, go-with-the-flow types of people, so it's only appropriate for them to be a neutral color such as gray because it can go with anything. Just as there are many shades of gray, from the light pink-gray of clouds, to the silvery-blue gray of pebbles, to the dark charcoal gray of slate, so too are there many different types of NINEs. In this section, we will also unpack some of the nuances of how you are a unique and particular NINE, unlike any other NINE the world has ever seen. Finally, we will explore triads, stances, subtypes, and wings, and along the way, we will prompt you to dig deeper into what shade of NINE you are.

SHADES OF NINE

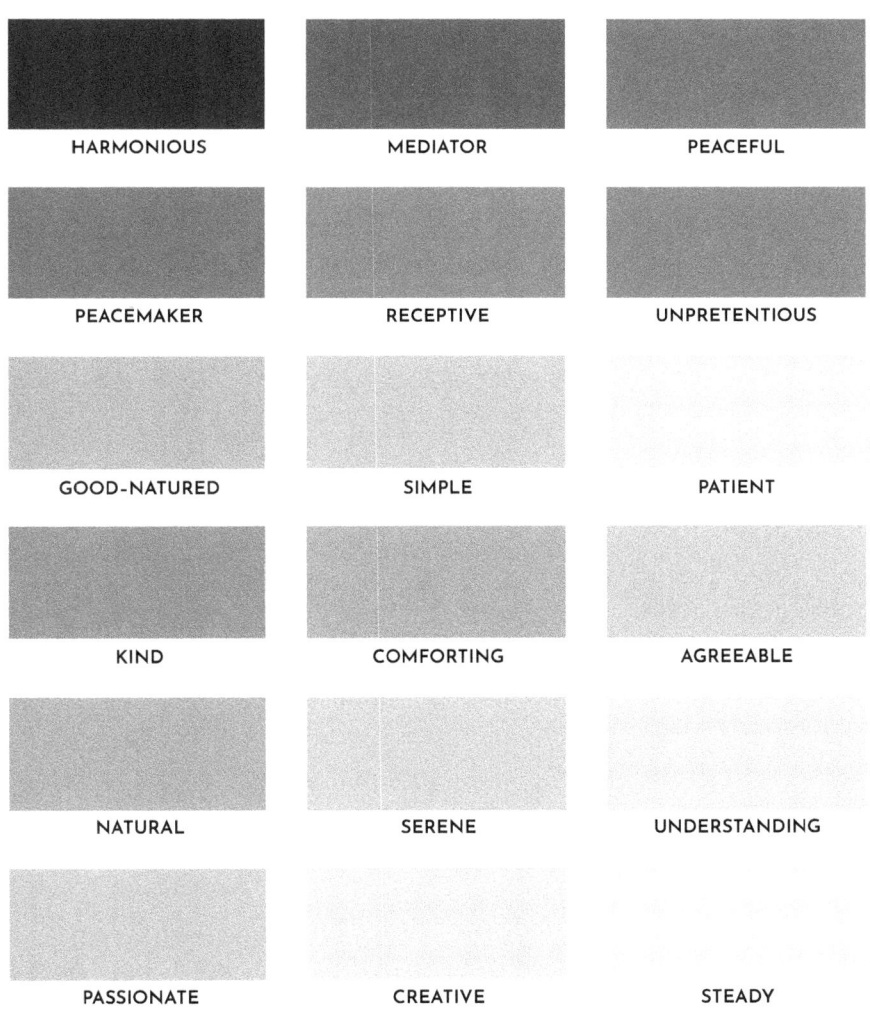

HARMONIOUS	MEDIATOR	PEACEFUL
PEACEMAKER	RECEPTIVE	UNPRETENTIOUS
GOOD-NATURED	SIMPLE	PATIENT
KIND	COMFORTING	AGREEABLE
NATURAL	SERENE	UNDERSTANDING
PASSIONATE	CREATIVE	STEADY

BODY TRIAD

NINEs are in the Body Triad, meaning they take in information intuitively through their bodies. Their first reaction, even if it's instantaneous, is a physical one. NINEs have strong gut feelings about what to do, even if they don't always act on them.

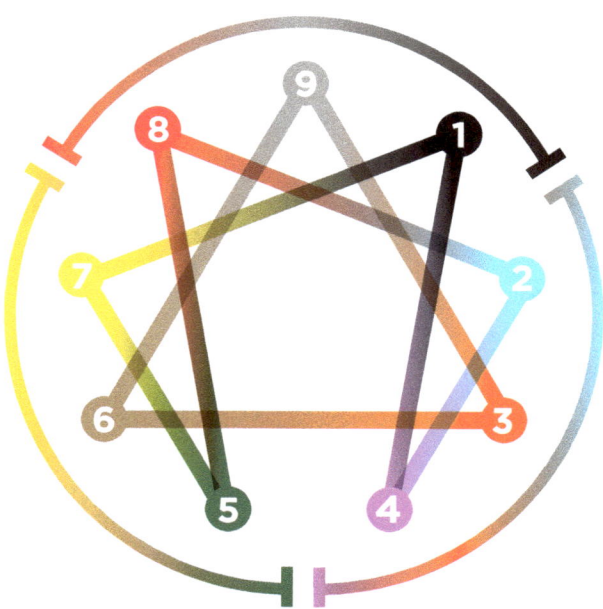

➤ Does this description apply to you? Is there anything that highly
resonates with you?

_____

_____

_____

_____

_____

_____

_____

➤ Is there anything you strongly disagree with? What is it? How do
you experience things differently?

_____

_____

_____

_____

_____

_____

_____

_____

➤ Have you ever you felt physically ill, only to discover that the source of your illness was actually relational conflict at work or home? Something you were avoiding?

_____

_____

_____

_____

_____

_____

_____

➤ What would it look like for you to practice assertiveness, not aggression?

_____

_____

_____

_____

_____

_____

_____

_____

_____

As a part of the Body Triad, NINEs feel emotions physically, especially feeling all the tension that they place on themselves. One emotion to pay attention to is anger, which is a motivating factor for all three types in the Body Triad. NINEs are often described as being asleep to their anger. They ignore or suppress their anger, feeling that it would take less energy to suppress it than act on it. NINEs fall asleep to their anger subconsciously most of the time, which can look like realizing that they're angry minutes, hours, or even days after the event that triggers their anger. Sometimes NINEs realize that they're angry when they feel it somewhere in their bodies.

➤ **Can you think of a time when you "fell asleep" to, or suppressed, your anger? How does anger show up in your body? What does it feel like?**

_____

_____

_____

_____

➤ **When in the past have you successfully been able to identify the source of your anger? What holds you back from engaging with your anger?**

_____

_____

_____

_____

Anger is not considered to be a primary emotion but a secondary emotion. Secondary emotions are those caused by another emotion. This means that when you feel anger, it is likely caused by another emotion first. Anger is not a "negative" emotion; there is no such thing. Emotions are nothing more than your body communicating with you to pay attention, to wake up.

➤ **Does reframing anger in this way help you think differently about anger?**

_____

_____

_____

_____

_____

➤ **The past few times that you have felt angry, which primary emotions were causing your anger? Were you anxious, scared, hurt, sad, frustrated, nervous, or embarrassed? What would it look like for you to tolerate feelings without shutting down or erupting in anger?**

_____

_____

_____

_____

_____

_____

WITHDRAWING STANCE

NINEs are in the Withdrawing Stance. They are oriented away from other people, with a strong tendency to retreat inward. NINEs live much of their lives in their own internal worlds, their inner sanctum. They can easily get lost in their own thoughts, live entire scenarios in their imaginations, and even settle or resolve conflict with others without actually communicating with them.

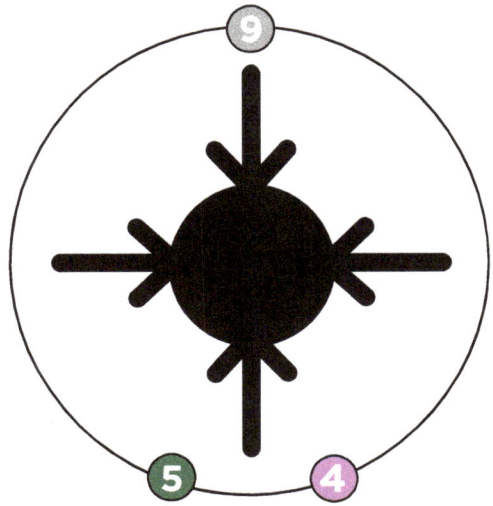

➤ Does this description apply to you? Is there anything that highly resonates with you?

_____

_____

_____

_____

_____

_____

_____

➤ Is there anything you strongly disagree with? What is it? How do you experience things differently?

_____

_____

_____

_____

_____

_____

_____

➤ When was the last time you retreated to your imagination or your inner sanctum? What triggered your retreat?

_____

_____

_____

_____

_____

_____

_____

➤ What does your internal world look and feel like? Is it a safe place? Is this the place you go when others tell you that you have the one-hundred-mile stare? Describe it here.

_____

_____

_____

_____

_____

_____

_____

_____

NINEs also withdraw to preserve their own sense of autonomy, especially if anyone tries too hard to force them into anything. We refer to all three types in the Withdrawing Stance as "doing-repressed," meaning that they think and feel more intuitively than they "do" or act. They often are deep, brilliant, sensitive minds whose primary struggle is involving themselves and imposing their will on the environment around them. Even though NINEs are in the Body Triad, they are still doing-repressed. They have physical, gut responses to situations, but their default next step is to suppress rather than to move into action.

➤ **Have you ever had the experience of feeling stuck or inactive in the face of a decision, big or small? Do you ever find yourself withdrawing or going on autopilot rather than being present in the moment?**

_____

_____

_____

_____

_____

_____

_____

_____

_____

_____

_____

➤ Has your tendency to withdraw ever had an impact on your relationships with those around you?

_____

_____

_____

_____

_____

_____

_____

_____

_____

_____

_____

Those in the Withdrawing Stance also have an orientation toward the past rather than a focus on the future or the present moment. They may replay old conversations, focus on "the way things were," and feel powerless to repair the bad or improve the good. This can lead to the inaction we mentioned previously.

➤ **When did you last find yourself replaying a past scenario? Why were you replaying this scenario?**

_____

_____

_____

_____

_____

_____

➤ **What would it take for you to learn to become grounded in the present moment?**

_____

_____

_____

_____

_____

_____

WINGS

Some NINEs have a very strong wing, while some find that they have balanced wings or no wing at all. NINEs with an EIGHT wing (9w8) live in a constant tension between a desire to keep the peace and a desire to rock the boat about whatever injustice they're facing. They can feel at times as if they are two different people that go back and forth between who's controlling their words and actions. 9w8s are generally more assertive, outwardly passionate, and antiauthoritarian than 9w1s.

NINEs with a ONE wing (9w1) also live in constant tension between the desire to be unbothered by life and a desire to right all of the wrongs that they encounter, which inevitably requires action and inconveniencing themselves. They are generally more inwardly focused, idealistic, orderly, and dutiful than 9w8s. 9w1s usually have some sort of outlet for their organizing. Their go-with-the-flow personalities often have a couple areas where they are more rigid and structured.

9W8   9W1

> Of these descriptions of 9w8 and 9w1, does one resonate more strongly with you? In what way?

_____

_____

_____

_____

_____

> If you have a wing, how do you find that your wing (w8, w1, or balanced) shades your NINE-ness?

_____

_____

_____

_____

_____

_____

➤ How does your wing balance you?

_____

_____

_____

_____

_____

_____

_____

_____

➤ When do you find yourself tapping into your wing? What does it
provide for you?

_____

_____

_____

_____

_____

_____

_____

_____

SUBTYPES

One part of the Enneagram that unlocks a whole lot of clarity is the subtypes, or instincts. Each person is dominant in one of three instincts: Self-Preservation (SP), Sexual (SX), or Social (SO). That instinct within your type is your subtype. Each person also has a secondary subtype and will likely find that one of the three instincts does not relate to them. For example, a NINE could be a SO/SX NINE, meaning their dominant subtype is Social and their secondary subtype is Sexual.

Self-Preservation (SP) NINE: SP NINEs are more inclined toward routines than the other NINE subtypes. They love very tangible things that bring them comfort, whether that be eating, sleeping, exercising, or reading. The stereotype of NINEs wanting to live entirely within their cozy little worlds with lots of warm laughter, good food, peace, and quiet is most descriptive of SP NINEs. SP NINEs find comfort in their routines because routines are their way of engaging with life in a predictable manner, minimizing the energy that new challenges require. SP NINEs can become frustrated and irritable when their rhythms are interrupted and they need to expend their energy on unwanted challenges.

Sexual (SX) NINE: SX NINEs crave intensity and adventure and are more excitable than the other NINE subtypes. They are also more prone toward merging, and they do so deeply with a handful of close relationships. SX NINEs can feel, explore, and live vicariously through these significant relationships in their lives and have a harder time being alone. They can easily vacillate between feeling wild and adventurous and wanting to retreat back inside their shells. While SP NINEs can lose themselves in their routines, SX NINEs can lose themselves in close relationships.

Social (SO) NINE: Many SO NINEs do not present like other NINEs at all because of their inclination toward whole groups of people. They can come across as SEVEN-ish, as people see them as lighthearted and natural at floating around social groups. SO NINEs can gravitate toward central roles in groups for the sake of mediating or bringing people together, forgetting themselves in the process. They are the countertype, meaning they don't approach slothfulness the same way that SX and SP NINEs do. Rather than letting slothfulness overtake them physically, they suppress and avoid internal problems by busying themselves physically and socially. They act as though if they bring peace and harmony to the people around them, that will somehow eventually come into their internal worlds as well.

➤ As you read through these subtypes, which one is your dominant type? How do you know?

_____

_____

_____

_____

_____

_____

_____

_____

➤ Which is your secondary subtype? How do you know?

_____

_____

_____

_____

_____

_____

_____

_____

➤ Which of these subtypes does not resonate with you? How do you know?

_____

_____

_____

_____

➤ Which part of the description of each subtype resonated most strongly with you? How has your subtype shaded the sort of NINE you are?

_____

_____

_____

_____

_____

➤ Do you see your subtype as a hindrance or a help? Why?

_____

_____

_____

_____

_____

PART III

RELATIONSHIPS
AS A TYPE NINE

YOU AND EACH TYPE

Before we talk about the relationships between NINEs and each type, it's worth noting that this space is completely insufficient to fully explore them. Entire books have been written solely on relationships between types and how the Enneagram can affect each relationship. This table is here to get you thinking about some potential connection points and tension points that you can encounter with each type, including fellow NINEs.

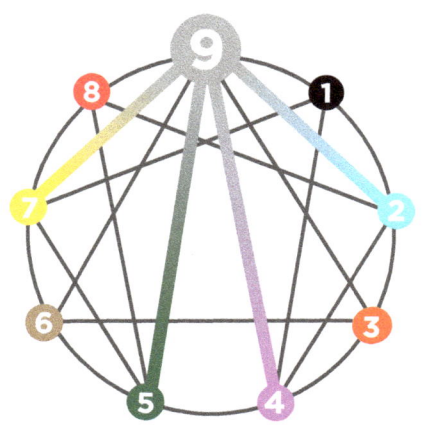

Relationship between NINE and ...	Potential places of synergy/connection	Potential places of conflict/tension
1	If a NINE and a ONE can be on the same page about any given topic, they can be very productive and balance each other well. NINEs can help ONEs embrace nuance and rest, and ONEs can help NINEs be objective and decisive. NINEs at their best can be stabilizing forces in the life of a ONE. Both types are also in the Body (or Gut) Triad, so they are both intuitive types who can understand each other on an instinctual level.	Both can be very stubborn. NINEs are immovable, and ONEs are rigid. ONEs live in black and white and NINEs live in gray, so they may frustrate the other with their opposing ways of seeing life.
	Both are generous and empathetic and naturally make great, supportive friends. They feel other peoples' feelings and make each other feel understood in ways that other types can't. They will always put the needs of the other before their own.	Both types struggle with saying no, so maintaining boundaries in this relationship can be a struggle. They also can both avoid saying how they really feel without prompting, so resentment can build between them in their own ways. TWOs can overextend themselves toward others, while NINEs withdraw, which can make the TWO feel neglected and the NINE feel smothered.

Relationship between NINE and . . .	Potential places of synergy/connection	Potential places of conflict/tension
3	When they're in good places, NINEs and THREEs can bring out the best in each other. NINEs can help THREEs relax, while THREEs can help NINEs "wake up" and inspire them toward action. The peace that the NINE brings to the relationship can help the THREE better achieve their goals. Healthy THREEs can also champion NINEs who have a hard time raising their voice or promoting themselves.	THREEs are generally quick, decisive people who like to get things done, while NINEs are slower and more deliberative. THREEs can get frustrated or impatient with NINEs in this regard, while NINEs can feel rushed and pressured by THREEs. Their communication styles can be at odds with each other, leading to more tension. THREEs can also take up more space, which doesn't allow NINEs to fully show up.
4	Both types love escaping into other worlds, whether it's through their imagination or through reading, so these types have a way of understanding each other. They both can take a long time to express themselves, so they can be more patient with each other than other types can.	Both types are in the Withdrawing Stance, so tension can go unaddressed for a long time. Relationships involve proactivity, which isn't always the easiest for a FOUR or a NINE. NINEs can become tired by the FOUR's endless ability to describe their emotions, and the FOUR can get frustrated by the NINE's difficulty expressing their own emotional depth.

Relationship between NINE and ...	Potential places of synergy/connection	Potential places of conflict/tension
 **5**	Both are good listeners who can take in a lot of what the other is saying without getting overwhelmed. Both ask great questions and are great at understanding. They can connect over their shared tendency to withdraw into their own mind castles/inner sanctums. They're both deep thinkers who can have great intellectual conversations if they have shared interests.	Similar to FOURs, FIVEs are also Withdrawing types who aren't naturally proactive, so there can be struggles with being truly present with one another. Both types usually keep their cards close to their chests, so it can take a while to build real emotional intimacy. They both get easily lost inside their own heads, which can distract them from the other who is right in front of them.
6	NINEs and SIXes often gravitate toward each other. NINEs exude the calm that SIXes long for, and SIXes can help bring NINEs into the present moment with their hypervigilance. SIXes make NINEs feel cared for, and they pay attention to things that NINEs wouldn't pay attention to for themselves. All three types in the Anchor Triad (THREE, SIX, and NINE) are used to conforming to the world around them, so they can easily meet the needs of the other. Both types are in the middle of their triads and are used to straddling fences.	If they are unhealthy or unaware, both types have tendencies to rely heavily on the other. NINEs merge with other people and forget themselves in the process, and SIXes build people deeply into their own security blankets, so if there is a disruption in that system, then they themselves are no longer okay. They can both lose themselves in the process. In stress, the hypervigilance of the SIX and the apparent lack of vigilance from the NINE can easily rub each other the wrong way.

Relationship between NINE and . . .	Potential places of synergy/connection	Potential places of conflict/tension
7	Both are adaptable and easy-going. SEVENs and NINEs are two of the easiest types on the Enneagram to get along with, so both can be very fun. They are both great at telling you what you want to hear, so people in this relationship can easily hype each other up.	Both types avoid conflict and hard conversations as much as they can, so this leaves plenty of room for tension to build under the surface. Both types are prone to ignore that tension even within themselves, but it's right there once they start to look for it. SEVENs in all of their energy and excitement can easily plow over a NINE who isn't ready or able to express that they're not on board with whatever the SEVEN is doing.
	Both types are very "what you see is what you get," so there is a helpful familiarity between the two where they won't have to guess what their real motives are. You know that you're always getting the real thing.	Similar to the relationship with ONEs, both types can be very stubborn. NINEs are immovable and EIGHTs are very headstrong, which can lead to some challenging relationships. If they get started on the wrong foot and the NINE is unwilling to comply with the EIGHT's will, deep resentment can quickly build between the two.

Relationship between NINE and . . .	Potential places of synergy/connection	Potential places of conflict/tension
	Naturally, two NINEs in any sort of relationship would "get" each other. They are easy to get along with, they love to have fun and enjoy themselves, and they're generally low-maintenance people to be around. Neither would bring up anything controversial, so they both know how to keep the mood pleasant. They are deep thinkers who can have a lot to say if given the space to do so, and NINEs are great at giving each other space.	Two NINEs in a relationship can tend toward stagnancy if neither is intentional about bringing up challenging or possibly controversial topics. NINEs can bottle things up rather than express their anger or frustration with any given situation, so there's a good possibility that conflict could go unaddressed much longer than is appropriate.

➤ As you read through these relationship prompts, can you think of any relationships in which you feel that you are misunderstanding each other? How can you connect better?

_____

_____

_____

_____

➤ Does this give language to any places of conflict that you're experiencing with another person? How do you think the Enneagram explains this particular tension?

_____

_____

_____

_____

➤ Are there people of a certain type in your life who you don't "get"? How can your relationship grow from better understanding this dynamic?

_____

_____

_____

_____

RIPPLE EFFECTS

As we say in our first book, *What's Your Enneatype?*, your actions and tendencies have an influence on more people than just you. It's better for everyone when you pay attention to the influence of your actions. These questions are designed to help you think about and become more aware of the ripple effects of your NINE-ish behaviors.

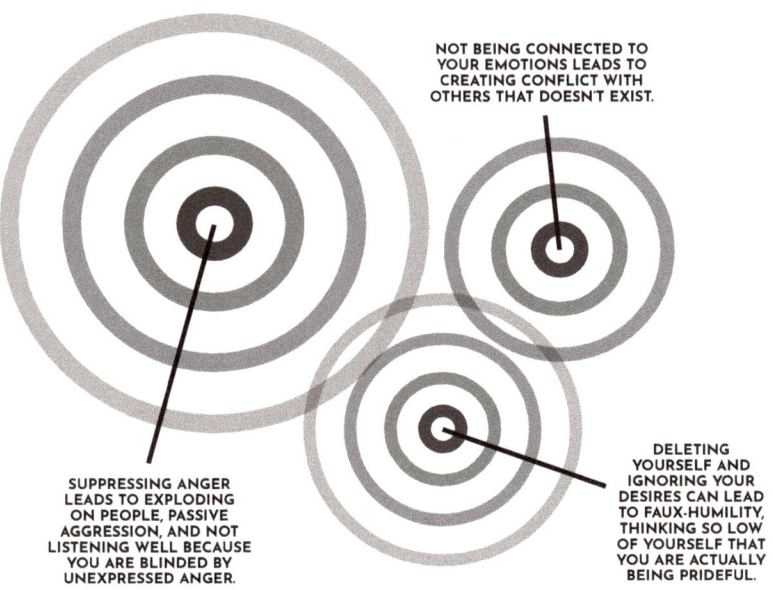

NOT BEING CONNECTED TO YOUR EMOTIONS LEADS TO CREATING CONFLICT WITH OTHERS THAT DOESN'T EXIST.

SUPPRESSING ANGER LEADS TO EXPLODING ON PEOPLE, PASSIVE AGGRESSION, AND NOT LISTENING WELL BECAUSE YOU ARE BLINDED BY UNEXPRESSED ANGER.

DELETING YOURSELF AND IGNORING YOUR DESIRES CAN LEAD TO FAUX-HUMILITY, THINKING SO LOW OF YOURSELF THAT YOU ARE ACTUALLY BEING PRIDEFUL.

➤ Is there any conflict that you're currently avoiding? What would be the cost of facing this conflict? What is the cost of not facing it?

_____

_____

_____

_____

➤ What are some conflicts that you settled internally on your own? Do you know if the other party feels resolution? How did things end from their point of view?

_____

_____

_____

_____

➤ Who pays the price when you hold back your true feelings? Why do you think others actually want to know what you think?

_____

_____

_____

_____

_____

➤ What do you do when you are bothered by a certain situation but don't express it? What is going on internally? Do others know that you're not happy? What steps do they take toward you?

_____

_____

_____

_____

_____

_____

➤ With whom have you been (intentionally or unintentionally) playing "hard to get" lately? What are you telling yourself about what they think of you? How can you ease any doubts that your absence might be causing them?

_____

_____

_____

_____

_____

_____

PART IV

THE WAY FORWARD AS A TYPE NINE

This final section will help you find a way forward. We believe that the goal of a tool like the Enneagram is not to put you in a box but to help you identify the box you have been living in and find a way out. We hope that the first three sections of this workbook have helped you identify what that box looks like and that this final section will help you begin to map the way forward: to unlearn the box of NINE, move beyond the labels, and find your way into a flourishing life unencumbered by the burdens of peace-keeping and conflict avoidance.

FALSE SELF/TRUE SELF

Earlier in this guide, we walked you through your NINE origin story: How did you become a NINE? What caused you to learn NINE-ness? In this section, we want to dig deeper into your False Self to uncover your True Self. We will examine your autopilot behaviors, coping strategies, and reactions to your fears and insecurities that have formed something called your False Self.

NINE's False Self often sounds like this:

➤ "If I ignore this instead of confronting it, I won't ever have to deal with it."

➤ "Nobody actually cares what I have to say. I have nothing to contribute." (Then the NINE often will look for evidence in others' actions to back up this False Self lie.)

➤ "People who create conflict aren't worth my time."

➤ "I'm not passionate enough to do anything big or meaningful."

➤ "I'm not upset. Everything is fine." (Then the NINE will often numb/ignore feelings and emotions, thus removing themselves from the narrative.)

➤ Which of these quotes from the NINE's False Self sounds most familiar to you?

_____

_____

_____

_____

_____

_____

_____

_____

➤ Are there any that do not resonate with you?

_____

_____

_____

_____

_____

_____

_____

_____

Spend some time challenging your False Self by asking these questions and writing your responses.

➤ How much energy does it take to always evade and ignore problems? What is the cost of these behaviors to yourself? To others?

_____

_____

_____

_____

_____

_____

➤ What are you afraid that conflict will do to you? What does engaging in conflict say about you? What is conflict?

_____

_____

_____

_____

_____

_____

_____

➤ What price do you make others pay when you delete yourself from the equation?

_____

_____

_____

_____

_____

_____

_____

➤ What would happen if you paid attention to your inner volcano rather than constantly suppressing it? What would the ripple effects look like in the lives of those around you?

_____

_____

_____

_____

_____

_____

_____

➤ Is everything really fine? What if it isn't?

_____

_____

_____

_____

_____

_____

_____

_____

➤ What will happen if you rock the boat?

_____

_____

_____

_____

_____

_____

_____

_____

➤ Do you need to be the one to enter into the tension? How do you know when you're taking up the peace-making work that is meant for someone else?

_____

_____

_____

_____

_____

_____

_____

➤ How can you tell when you're operating out of your False Self?

_____

_____

_____

_____

_____

_____

_____

_____

UNLEARNING

As you have been unpacking what your unique shade of NINE looks like, you have likely uncovered some of the beautiful, life-giving, flourishing aspects of what it means to be a NINE. Spend some time reviewing your answers to the questions in this guide and then reflect.

➤ What is your favorite part of being a NINE? What aspect of being a type NINE is most life-giving?

_____

_____

_____

_____

_____

_____

➤ What is the biggest gift of NINE-ness? Ask this same question of some of your closest people and document their answers as well.

_____

_____

_____

_____

_____

_____

_____

Likewise, you have probably identified some aspects of NINE-ness that are unhealthy behaviors and coping strategies. These things are no longer serving you and need to be unlearned.

➤ **What aspect of your NINE-ness is unhealthy and needs to be unlearned?**

_____

_____

_____

_____

_____

_____

➤ **What would change if you unlearned these things?**

_____

_____

_____

_____

_____

_____

_____

> What is the next positive step for you in unlearning these things?

_____

_____

_____

_____

_____

_____

_____

_____

_____

_____

PURPOSEFUL PRACTICES

Sometimes the practice of unlearning is easier when
you have disciplines, rhythms, and practices that
will help you as you take on this important work.

Below are some suggestions for you as you work on unlearning the shadow side of NINE and begin to silence the False Self.

Surrender: Surrender is a practice that frees us to let go of the burden of always needing to get our own way. NINEs are often unaware of all the anger and tension that they are holding, so the practice of naming and releasing these burdens will help NINEs truly find this peace. Practice spending time each morning sitting still with your hands open and palms facing up, breathing deeply and connecting with your body. Remind yourself of what is true and good. Let go of those things you cannot control.

Nature: If you are able, spend time in nature, which will help you restore balance and return to a sense of peace and calm. Walk trails, hike, bike, garden, or tend to indoor plants. Nature is a gift that reminds us that though we live in a world of chaos, there is a natural order to life. You can be reminded of how the world is much bigger than you and your current problems, and it always has been.

Peacemaking: Don't feel bad about your desire to help others resolve conflict. Look for ways to use this gift. It's a stretching practice for you because you have to enter in and involve yourself in the messiness of relationships, but it is also one of the most natural ways you can serve others around you. How can you mediate? Counsel? Encourage others? How can you be a peaceful, calm presence in an increasingly anxious world?

Fixed-Hour Prayer: This ancient practice of stopping routinely to re-center provides a soothing rhythm that will calm you down, reminding you of what is most urgent and important.

Stay Active: Make sure you stay active each day by moving your body to whatever degree you are able.

Listen: Everyone has needs, and everyone has desires. An important step in NINEs finding their own voice is identifying and claiming your needs. It can be as simple as writing down two or three simple needs or desires every day, but it's crucial for your growth that you make space to figure out what you want and what you need.

SELF-CARE FOR NINES

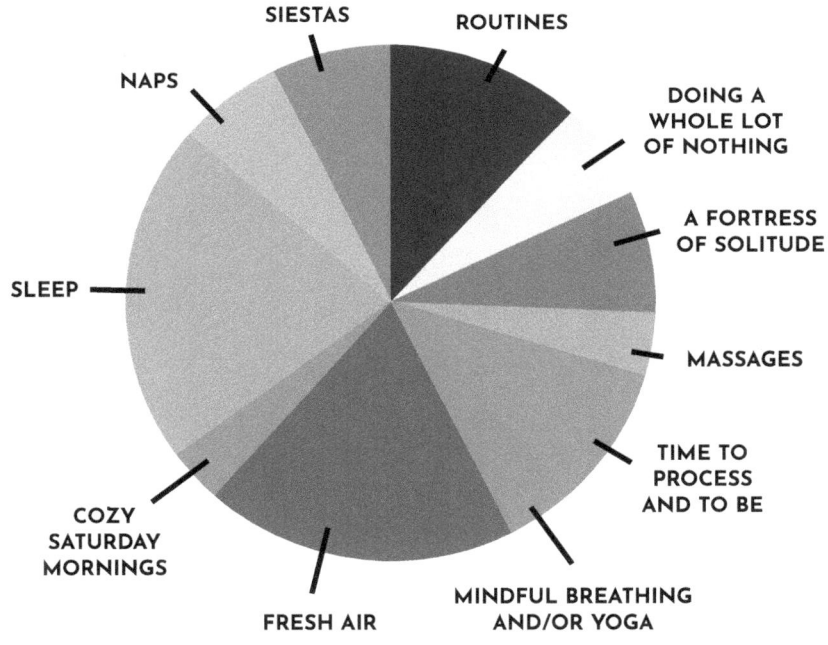

SIESTAS
ROUTINES
NAPS
DOING A WHOLE LOT OF NOTHING
A FORTRESS OF SOLITUDE
MASSAGES
SLEEP
TIME TO PROCESS AND TO BE
COZY SATURDAY MORNINGS
MINDFUL BREATHING AND/OR YOGA
FRESH AIR

➤ Which of the practices listed above are you already engaging with?

_____

_____

_____

_____

_____

_____

_____

➤ Which of the practices listed above sounds most challenging to you?
  Why do you think that is?

_____

_____

_____

_____

_____

_____

_____

➤ How is the practice of peace-making different from peace-faking or merely peace-keeping?

_____

_____

_____

_____

_____

_____

_____

➤ Is there a practice listed above, or perhaps something that is not listed, that you want to put into practice this week? What steps do you need to take to make that happen?

_____

_____

_____

_____

_____

_____

_____

_____

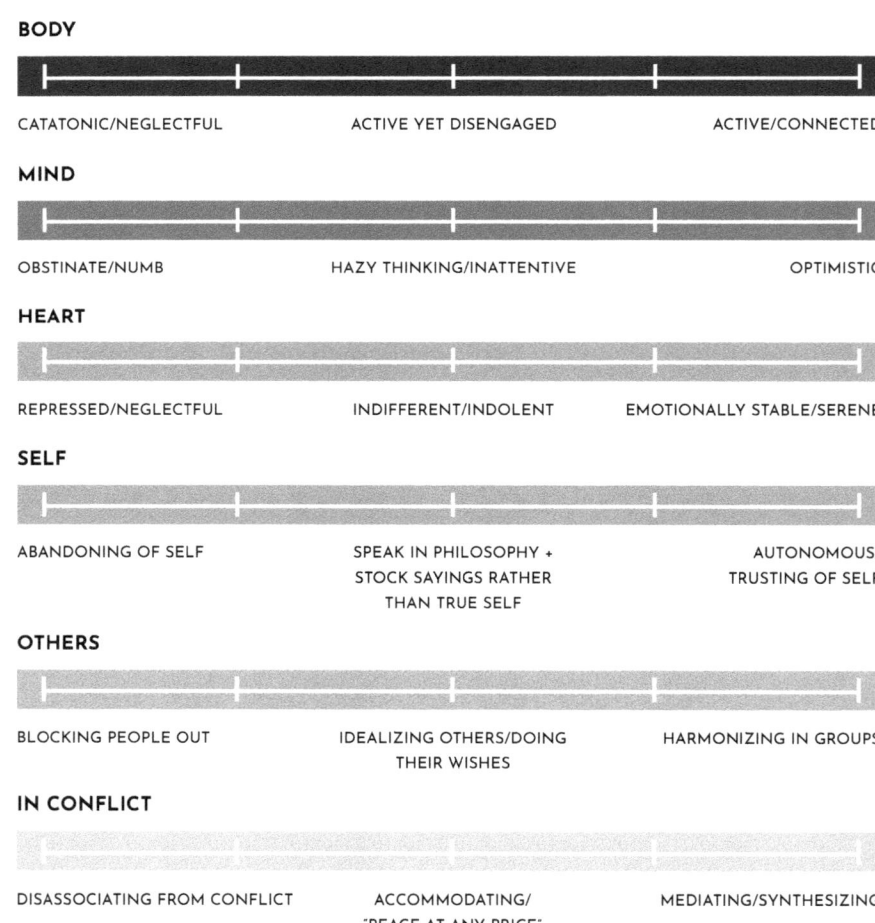

BODY

CATATONIC/NEGLECTFUL   ACTIVE YET DISENGAGED   ACTIVE/CONNECTED

MIND

OBSTINATE/NUMB   HAZY THINKING/INATTENTIVE   OPTIMISTIC

HEART

REPRESSED/NEGLECTFUL   INDIFFERENT/INDOLENT   EMOTIONALLY STABLE/SERENE

SELF

ABANDONING OF SELF   SPEAK IN PHILOSOPHY +   AUTONOMOUS/
                            STOCK SAYINGS RATHER   TRUSTING OF SELF
                            THAN TRUE SELF

OTHERS

BLOCKING PEOPLE OUT   IDEALIZING OTHERS/DOING   HARMONIZING IN GROUPS
                            THEIR WISHES

IN CONFLICT

DISASSOCIATING FROM CONFLICT   ACCOMMODATING/   MEDIATING/SYNTHESIZING
                                     "PEACE AT ANY PRICE"

YOUR NEXT STEPS

As this guide comes to an end, we hope that you spend some time in reflection about what your next steps need to be. NINEs who don't address their unhealthy patterns and habits can end up walking down a very dangerous road. They end up evading and avoiding all sorts of difficulties, numbing or narcotizing problems, or merging to the point that life begins to spiral downward into isolation, depression, and broken relationships. We are proud of you for taking steps toward unlearning the aspects of NINE-ness that are harmful and boldly expressing the aspects of NINE-ness that are a gift to the world.

Each day you will be faced with choices to continue your unconscious patterns or to step away from them toward decisive action. This will require that you look far into the horizon and choose hard-earned peace-making rather than instantaneous peace-faking or peace-keeping. You will have opportunities to take decisive action in small, simple ways every day. The more you choose this more difficult pursuit, the more you'll find yourself able to resolve, mediate, and reconcile bigger and bigger problems. The path to growth brings true harmony not only to you but to the world around you.

Dear NINE, you have the daily opportunity to have your deepest desire become your greatest gift to the world. And we hope you take it.

— *Liz and Josh*

NOTES

ABOUT THE AUTHORS

Liz Carver and **Josh Green** run one of the most popular Enneagram accounts on social media, **@justmyenneatype**. Liz is a designer and the director of communication at Eastbrook Church in Wisconsin, and Josh is a campus minister for InterVarsity Christian Fellowship. Together, they wrote *What's Your Enneatype?* Visit their website **justmyenneatype.wordpress.com** for more information.

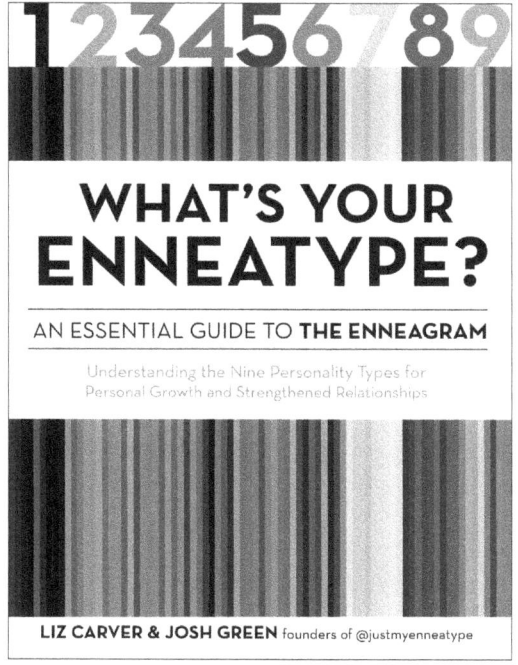

What's Your Enneatype?
978-1-5923-3952-5

INDEX

A
anger
as communication, 44
emotional tolerance
and, 44
engaging with, 43
identifying source of,
43, 44
motivation and, 43
suppression of, 43

B
Body Triad, 40-44

C
childhood wounds
beliefs, 35
developed tendencies, 34
lack of importance, 33
self-expression and, 33
variety of, 32
**color, characteristics of,
38-39**
conflict
assertiveness vs.
aggression, 42
avoidance of, 17, 19-20,
68, 75-78
disintegration and, 21
"doing-repressed," 48
engagement in, 20
internal resolution of,
45-46, 68
physical reaction to, 42
relationships and, 61-66
resolution, 45-46, 68, 84
ripple effects of, 68

verbalization of, 69
coping strategies, 14

D
disintegration
conflict avoidance
and, 21
SIXes and, 21
warning signs, 23-25
"doing-repressed," 48

E
EIGHTs
relationships with, 64
wings, 51-52
Enneadictionary
inner sanctum, 27-29
merging, 27-29, 31
numbing/narcotizing,
27-29, 30
one-hundred-mile stare,
27-29, 30

F
False Self
acknowledging, 78
challenge questions,
75-78
voice of, 73-74
**FIVEs, relationships
with, 63**
fixed-hour prayer, 84
**FOURs, relationships
with, 62**

H
harmony
as motivation, 14

Social (SO) subtype
and, 55

I
inner sanctum
definition of, 27-29
description of, 47
Withdrawing Stance
and, 45-46, 47
integration
signs of, 26
THREEs and, 26

L
love
avoidance of conflict
and, 17
tangible comfort, 55

M
merging
acknowledgment of, 31
definition of, 27-29
relationships and, 31
motivation
ego and, 16
harmony as, 14
verbalizing, 16

N
nature, 84
**needs, identification
of, 84**
numbing/narcotizing
acknowledgement
of, 30
definition of, 27-29

CPSIA information can be obtained
at www.ICGtesting.com
Printed in the USA
BVHW090613030522
635955BV00003B/107

9 780760 376737